THE A.B.C. of PIANO PLAYING

An Easy Method for Beginners

by

Boris Berlin

Book Three

Revised Edition

Including Elementary Technic for Beginners

Illustrations by Lida Koníček

Music Engraving and Typesetting by Musictype Limited

ISBN 0-88797-151-2

PREFACE

The A.B.C. of Piano Playing has been prepared to meet the ever-growing demand for a simple, yet progressive beginners' series for children.

The material included in this series has been divided into lessons, thus simplifying the assignment task of the teacher. Since children expect to play the piano right from the beginning, each lesson contains simple tunes which the pupil can play while learning about the keyboard and about notation. The Lessons in Writing correspond to the Lessons in Playing. They will prove invaluable as a "theory aid" in learning the pieces.

As in Books 1 and 2, many of the illustrations found in Book 3 of the A.B.C. of Piano Playing contain elements that relate to the corresponding pieces. Thus, in the 1st Lesson, a pattern in the curtain suggests the beginning of the second phrase; in the 2nd Lesson, the snowflakes and sun illustrate the left hand passage in measures 4-5 and 8-9; in the 3rd Lesson, the flowers are arranged in a pattern that parallels that of the notes in measures 3-4 and 7-8; and in the 5th Lesson, the flowers indicate the pattern of notes found from the end of measure 2 to the third beat of measure 4. Musical patterns may also be found in the illustrations for Lessons 6, 7, 9, 10, and 11.

Elementary Technic For Beginners, which includes a number of useful exercises, may be found at the end of this book.

As the A.B.C. of Piano Playing is not meant to be self-instructing, the presentation of its contents is left to the teacher.

FOR REFERENCE

THE KEYBOARD

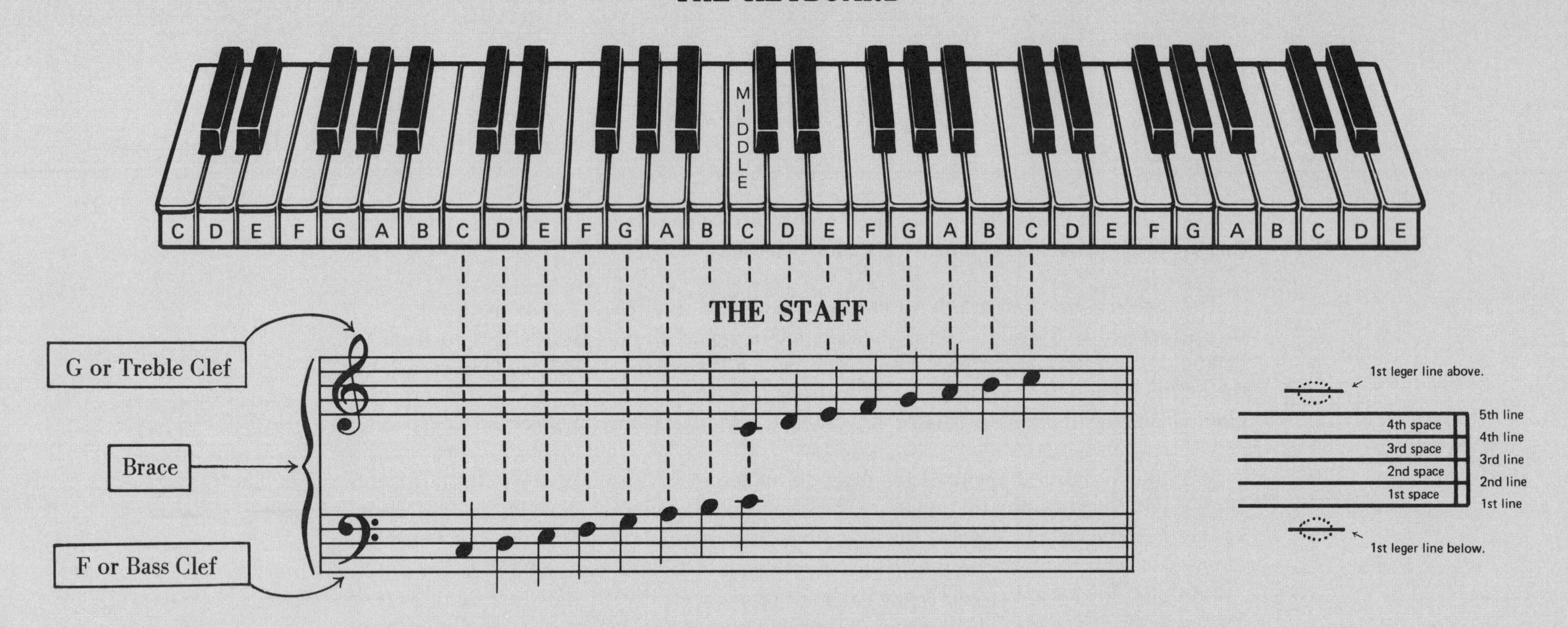

MARKS OF EXPRESSION AND OTHER MUSICAL SIGNS

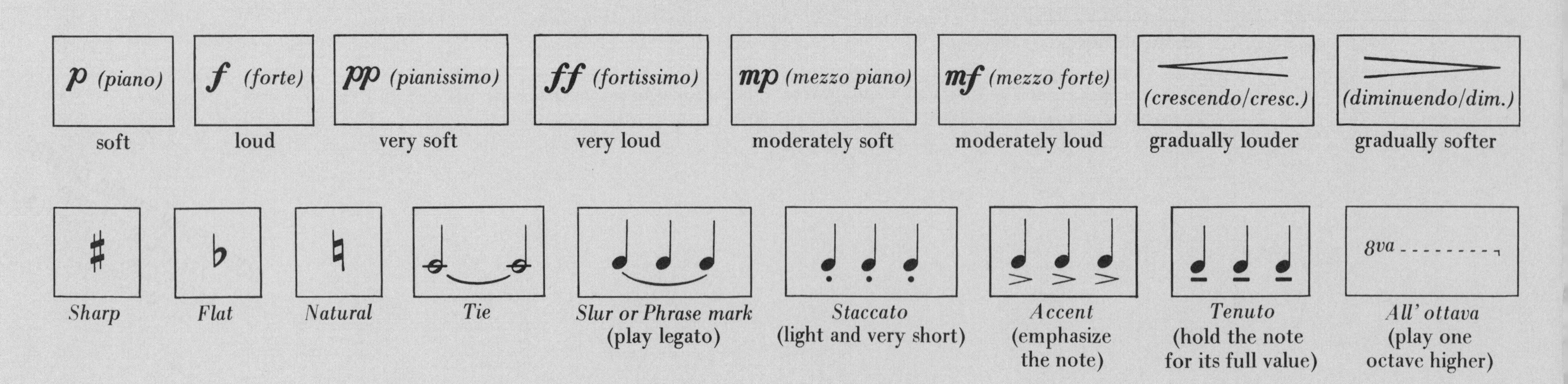

FOR REFERENCE

TIME VALUES

Whole Note (4 beats)
(Tah - ah - ah - ah)

Dotted Half Note (3 beats)
(Tah - ah - ah)

Half Note (2 beats)
(Tah - ah)

Dotted Quarter Note (1½ beats)
(Tah - i)

Quarter Note (1 beat)
(Tah)

Two Eighth Notes (½ beat each, two notes to 1 beat)
(Ti - ti)

Dotted Quarter Note (three eighth notes to 1 beat)
(Tah - i)

Three Eighth Notes (1 pulse each, three pulses to 1 beat)
(Ti - ti - ti)

NOTES AND RESTS

TIME SIGNATURES

2/4 3/4 4/4

The upper figure shows the number of *beats* to a measure.

The lower figure shows the kind of note to one beat. (The figure 4 represents a quarter note.)

6/8

The upper figure shows the number of *pulses* to a measure.

The lower figure shows the kind of note to one pulse. (The figure 8 represents an eighth note.)

1st LESSON IN WRITING

1. Fill in the blocks: 1 block for a 1-beat note, 2 blocks for a 2-beat note, 3 blocks for a 3-beat note, and ½ block for a ½-beat note.
   Write the number of beats (counts) under each block.

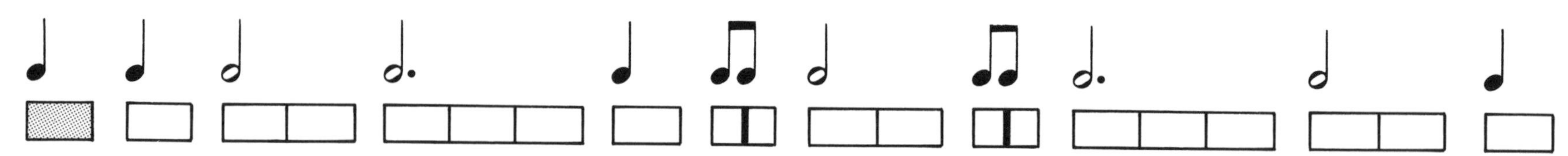

Number of beats: 1

2. Draw bar-lines to divide this tune into measures, then print the correct letter-name under each note.
   Draw arrows in the direction of note-patterns (a), (b), (c), (d), (e) and (f).

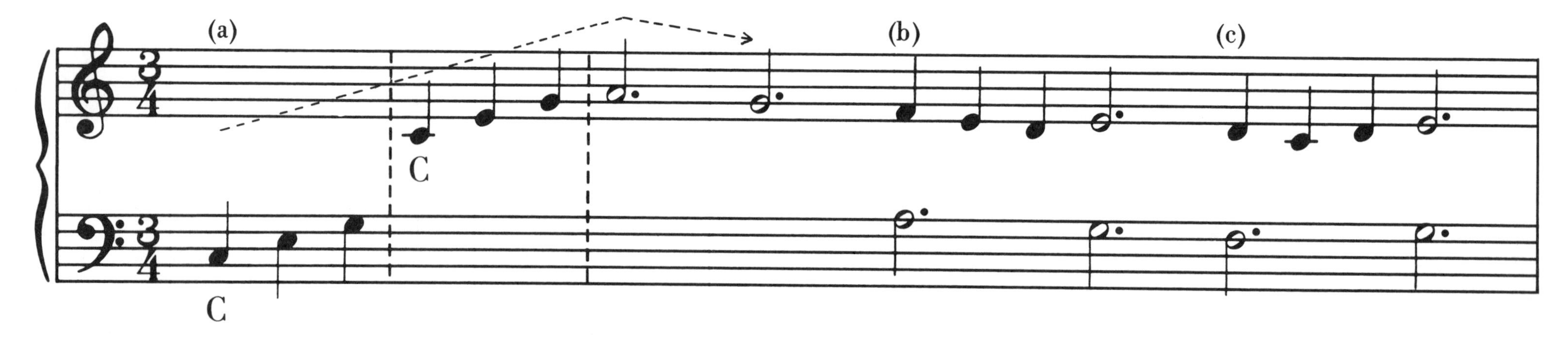

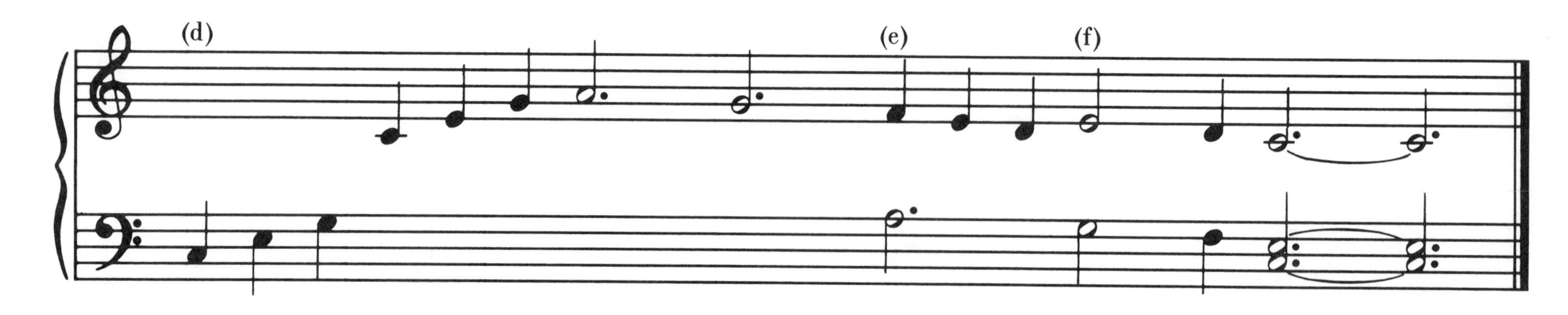

In measure 3 and measure 11, the left hand crosses over the right hand to play Treble A.
Remember: The Whole Rest indicates a measure of silence in *any* kind of time.

2nd LESSON IN WRITING

1. Draw notes on the staff for the keys marked X, then print the correct letter-name for each note in the space beneath the staves.

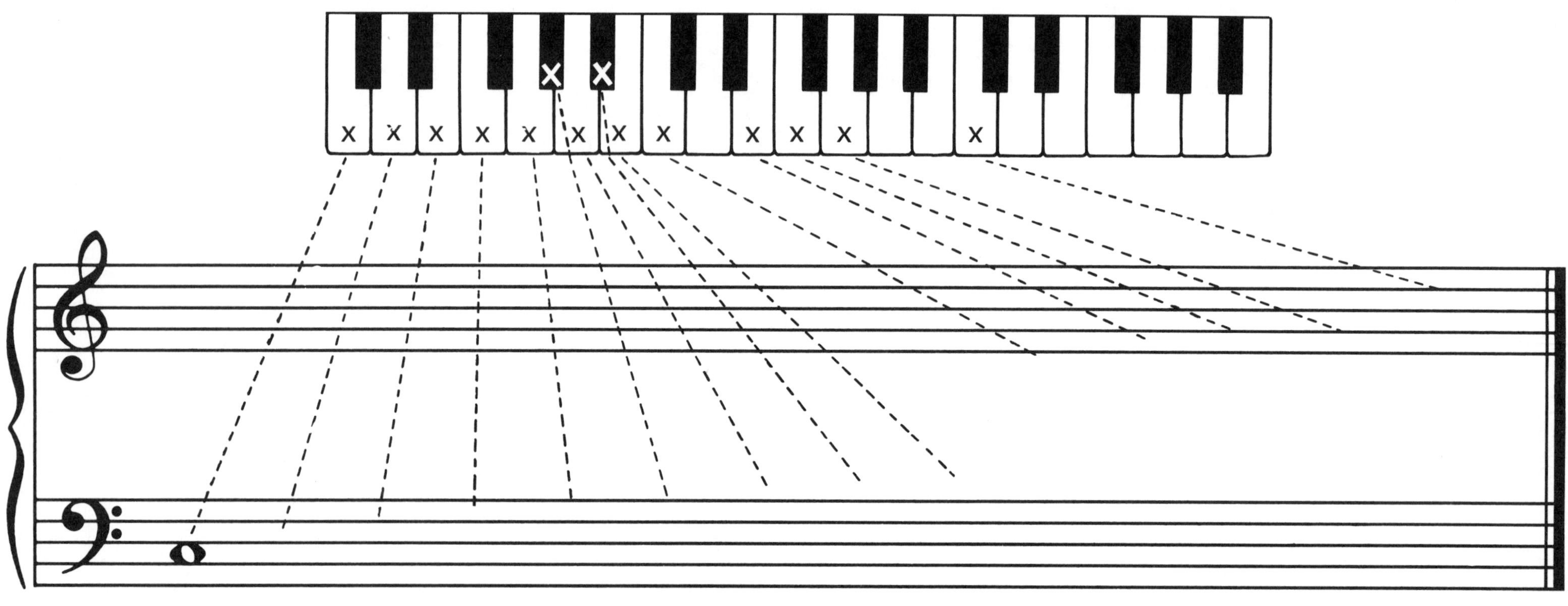

Letter-
names:

2. Add a time-signature to each of the following measures, then print the correct letter-name under each note.

Letter-
names:

Date . . . .

2nd LESSON

A Skating Waltz

What is the sign "♭" called? On which side of a note is it written?

3rd LESSON IN WRITING

1. Complete each measure by adding rests.

2. Draw a letter or sign for each of the following:

loud *(forte)* ____________ soft *(piano)* ____________ very loud *(fortissimo)* ____________ very soft *(pianissimo)* ____________

gradually softer *(diminuendo)* ____________________ gradually louder *(crescendo)* ____________________

3. Print the correct letter-name under each note, then write the counts for each measure in the space between the staves.
   Circle each pair of notes forming a skip (interval) of a THIRD.

Date . . . .
3rd LESSON
Count aloud and clap:
rit.
gradually slower
Cradle Song
Gently
French Folk Song
arr. B. B.
Bye - lo, hush - a - bye, See, the moon is in the sky.
rit.
Bye - lo, do not peep, Birds and ba - bies fall a - sleep.
What is a Phrase? What is an Accompaniment?
R.H.
Second Part
(for duets)
L.H.

4th LESSON IN WRITING

1. Draw bar-lines to divide this tune into measures, then print the correct letter-name under each note. Circle each pair of notes forming a skip (interval) of a FOURTH.

2. Draw the key-signature B flat indicating the key of F (treble B♭ on the 3rd line, bass B♭ on the 2nd line), then draw a note for each letter-name.

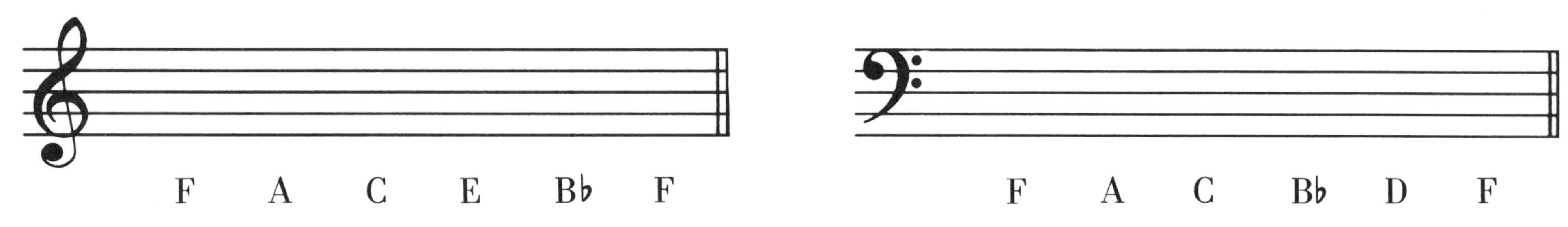

3. Use an X to mark the correct answer.

Can you tell the difference between a *staccato* and a *legato* touch? How many *staccato* dots are there in this piece?

5th LESSON IN WRITING

1. Draw notes that correspond to the given rests.

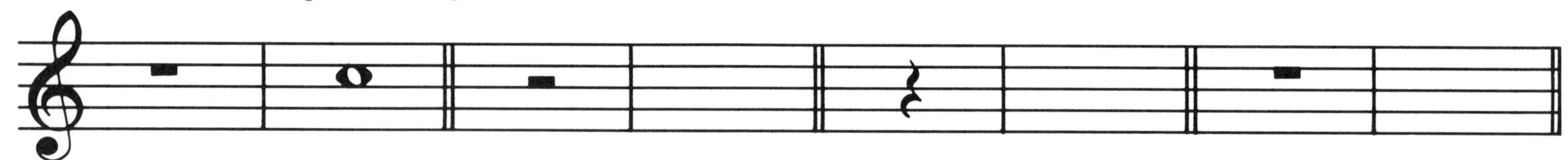

2. (a) Draw bar-lines to divide this tune into measures. Print the letter-name under each note, then write the counts for each measure in the space between the staves.
(b) Draw a slur (⌒) over or under each group of 3 notes forming a ♫ ♩ pattern. Then draw arrows in the direction of each 3-note pattern (UP, or DOWN).

3. Draw the key-signature F sharp indicating the key of G (treble F♯ on the 5th line, bass F♯ on the 4th line), then draw a note for each letter-name.

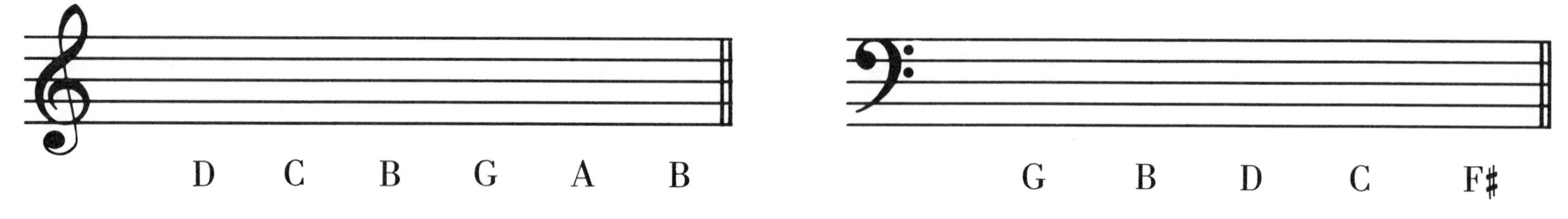

Be sure to observe the QUARTER RESTS.

6th LESSON IN WRITING

1. Fill in the blocks for the eighth notes, quarter notes, and dotted quarter notes.
Remember: 2 eighth notes equal 1 quarter note and 3 eighth notes equal 1 dotted quarter note.

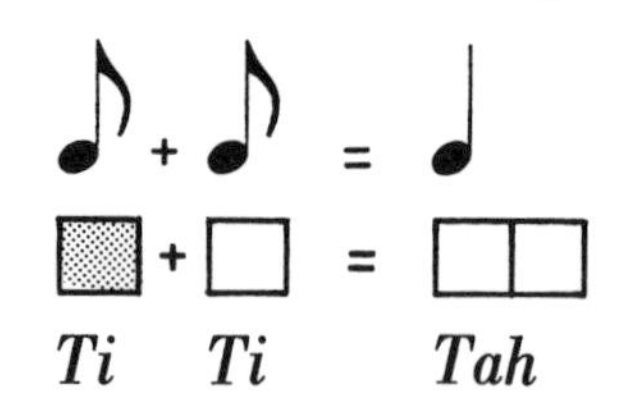

Ti Ti Ti Tah - i

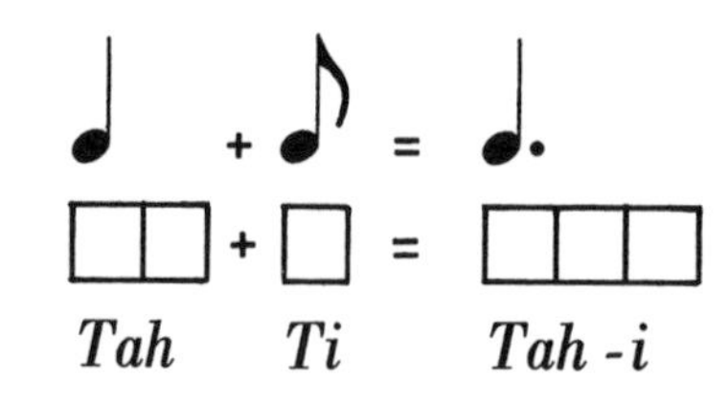

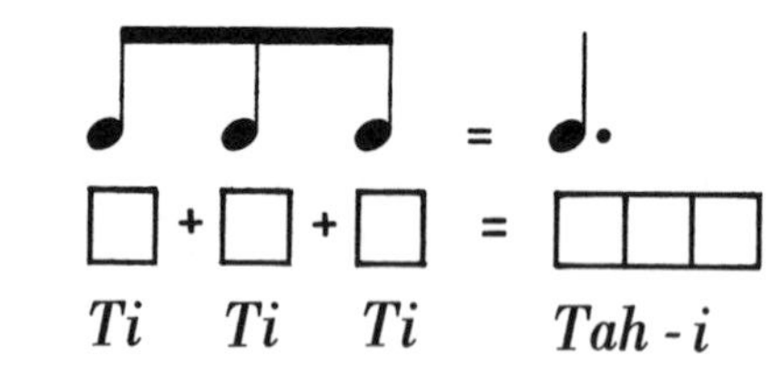

2. Copy the first 4 measures of the right-hand part of "A Canoe Trip". Print the correct letter-name under each note, then write the counts for each measure under the staff. Draw an arrow in the direction of each pattern of:

(a) notes moving UP and DOWN ; (b) repeated notes .

Letter-names: E F G

Counts: 1 2 3

3. Add the missing signs (dots, fingering, expression marks, etc.) from the left-hand part of "A Canoe Trip" to the notes shown below.

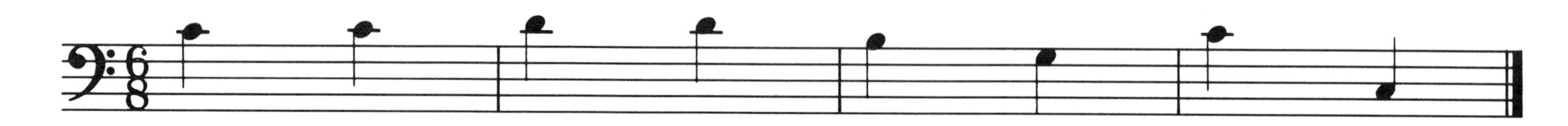

What is the sign "♯" called? On which side of a note is it written?

7th LESSON IN WRITING

1. Draw notes on the staff for the keys marked X, then print the correct letter-name for each note in the space beneath the staves. Notice that the first 8 notes form the scale of G.

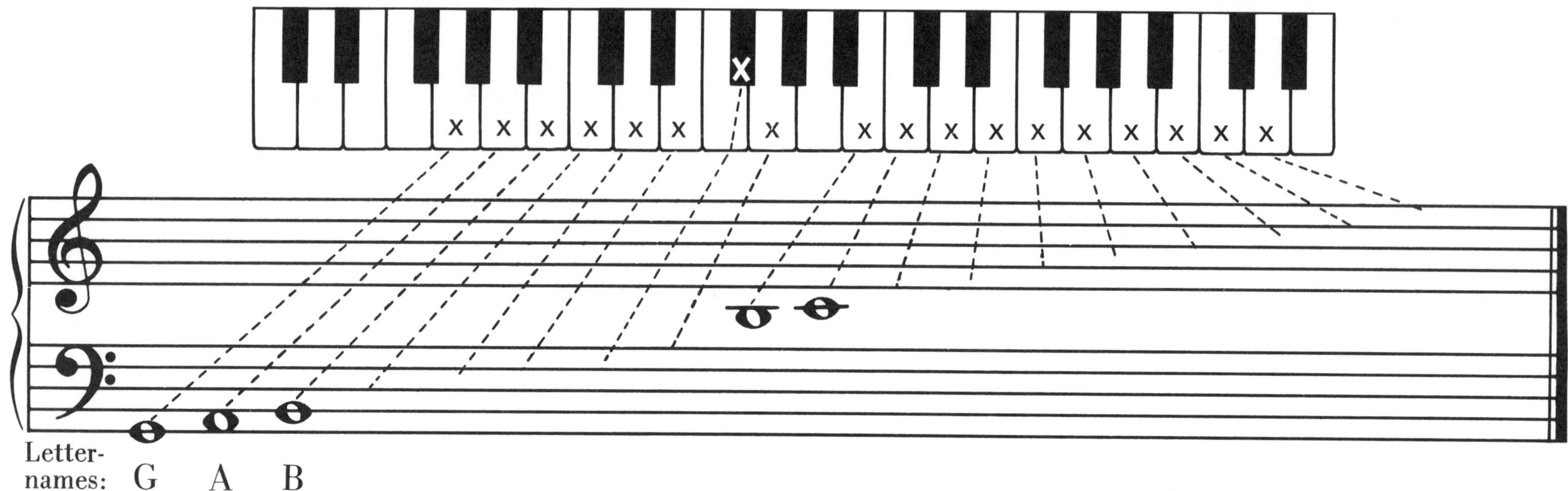

2. Use an X to mark the correct answer.

3. Draw an arrow in the direction of each pattern of notes moving (a) UP ; (b) DOWN ; (c) DOWN and UP ; (d) UP and DOWN . Write the counts for each measure beneath the staff.

Date . . . .
7th LESSON
Count aloud and clap:
1 2 3 1 2 3 1 2 3 1 2 3
Golden Slumbers
Slowly
arr. B. B.
p
mp
p
rit.
Do you know the words to this song? If so, try to sing them while playing the tune.

8th LESSON IN WRITING

1. Fill in the blocks for the eighth notes, quarter notes, and dotted quarter notes. Remember: 1 quarter note equals 2 eighth notes, and 1 dotted quarter note equals 3 eighth notes or 1 quarter note plus 1 eighth note.

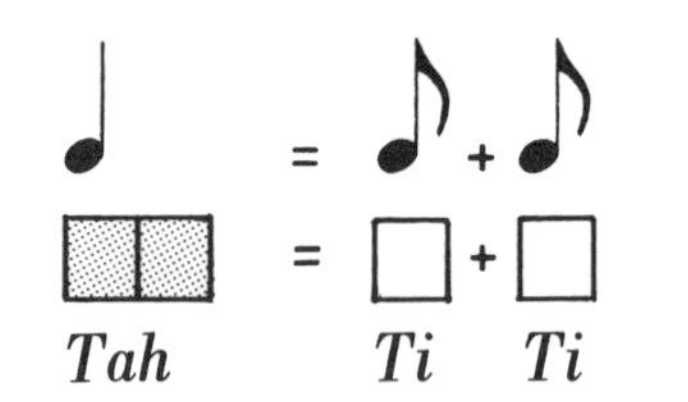

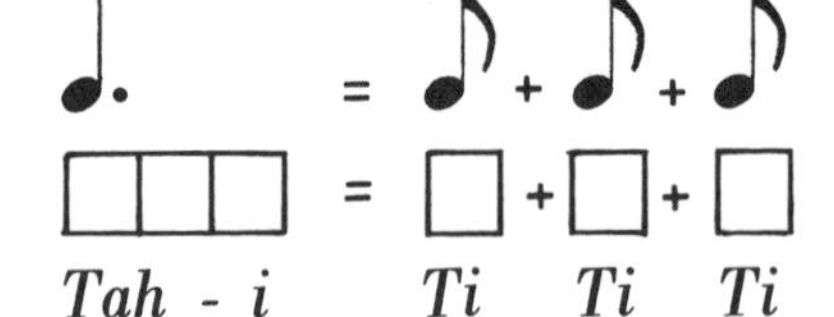

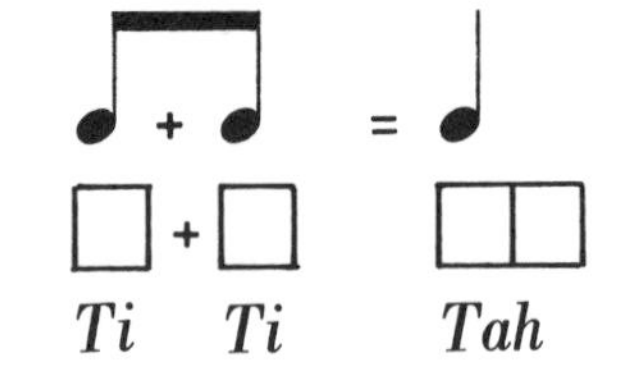

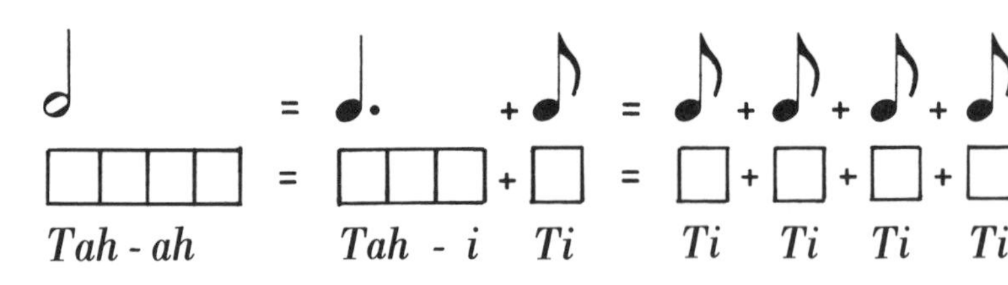

2. Add arrows in the direction of note-patterns (a), (b), (c), (d), and (e).
Use an X to mark the correct description of each pair of notes forming a skip (interval).

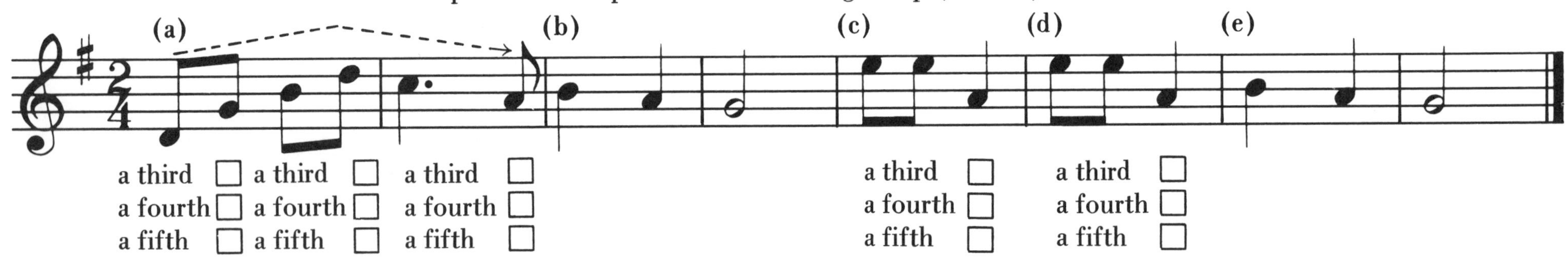

3. Draw a sign for each of the following:

tie 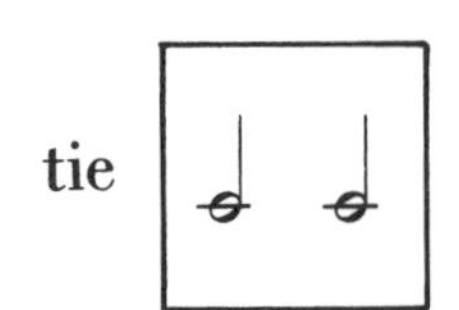 staccato  accent phrase mark  tenuto

4. What is the key signature of "Hop Scotch"? _____ How many THIRDS can you find in the left-hand part of "Hop Scotch"? _____
Circle all the THIRDS in the following excerpt.

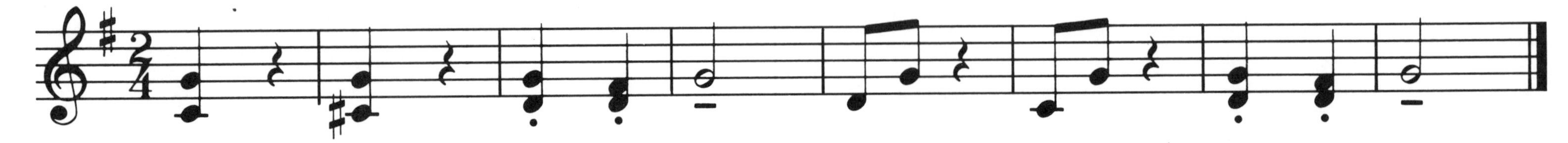

What is the KEY SIGNATURE of this piece? How many FOURTHS can you find in the L.H. part?
Note that both hands play in the Treble clef.

9th LESSON IN WRITING

1. Print the correct letter-name under each note, then write the counts for each measure in the space between the staves.

2. Fill in the blanks with the missing information from the melody shown below. Where necessary use an X to mark the correct answer. The melody begins with the note ___ in the ____ space and skips up to the note ___ in the ____ space. Together these 2 notes form an interval of a ____ . The 2nd measure consists of ___ notes which move UP ☐ DOWN ☐, from the note ___ to the note ___. The 3rd measure begins on the same note as measure ___. In measure 3, the melody skips from the note ___ to the note ___ on the ____ line, and the 2 notes form an interval of a ____.

3. Draw the notes of the scale of F. (Do not forget to add the key signature.)

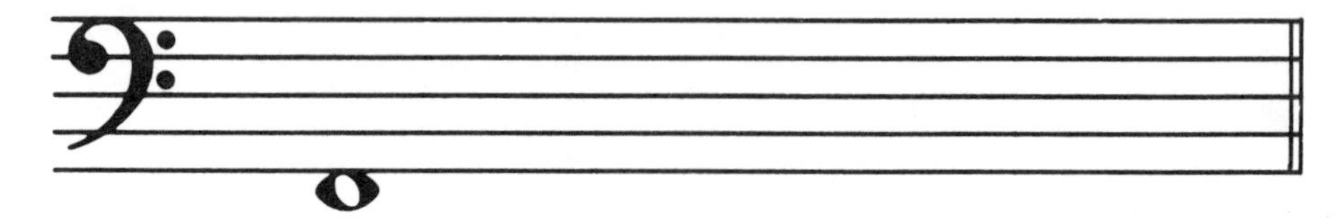

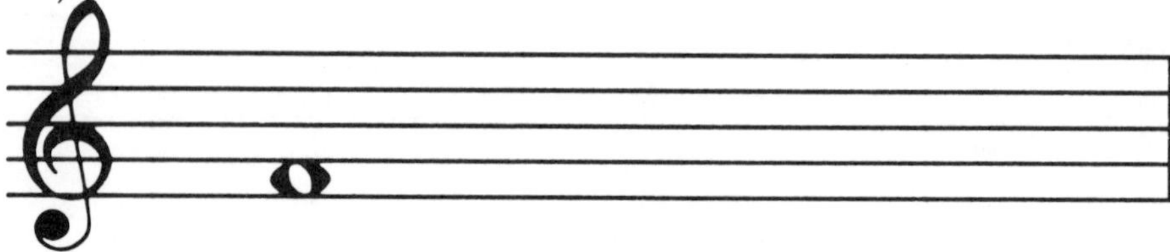

What is the KEY SIGNATURE of this piece? How many FOURTHS can you find in the L.H. part?

10th LESSON IN WRITING

1. Draw bar-lines to divide the following into measures. (The sign " 𝄾 " is an eighth rest.)

2. For each letter-name draw a note whose value corresponds to the number of beats shown beneath the staff.
Draw bar-lines to divide this tune into measures.

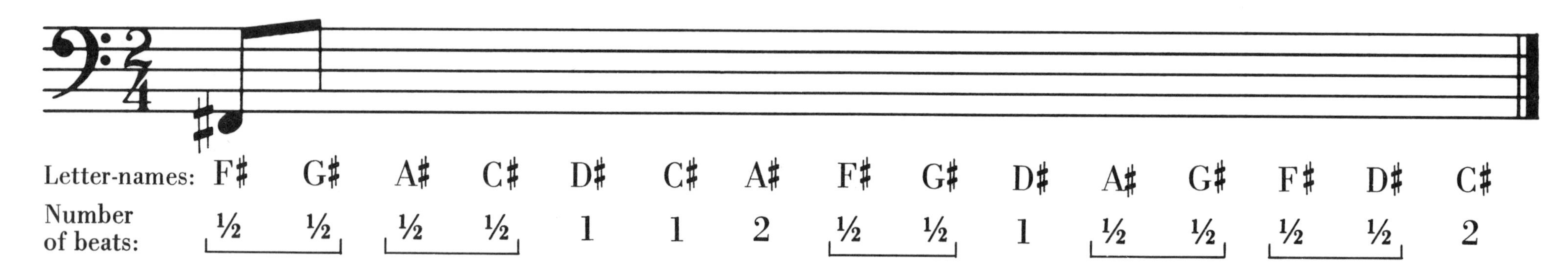

3. Print the correct letter-name under each note, then draw an arrow in the direction of each pattern of notes moving

Date . . . .

10th LESSON

Hallowe'en Pranks

Note the changes of clef in the left hand.

11th LESSON IN WRITING

1. Draw a line from each note on the staff to the corresponding key on this picture of the piano keyboard.
   Print the correct letter-name under each note.

2. Copy this rhythm, then clap it while counting the beats.

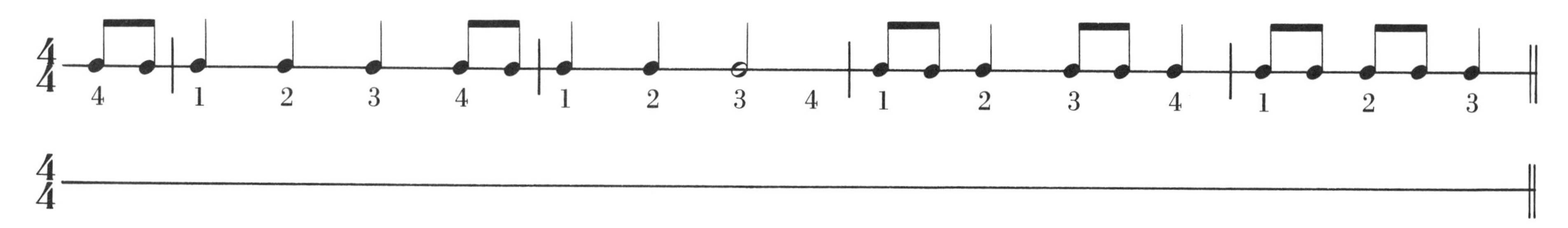

3. Make pairs of eighth notes by drawing STEMS and BEAMS. Print the correct letter-name under each note.

Which scale do these notes form? ______________

Date . . . .

11th LESSON

a tempo return to the original speed	*8va* - - ┐ play an octave higher

Old MacDonald Had a Farm

Note the G♯s and A♯s in the right-hand part. Play the BLACK KEY to the right of the G and to the right of the A.

12th LESSON IN WRITING

1. Fill in the blocks for the eighth notes, quarter notes, dotted quarter notes, half notes, and dotted half notes. Clap rhythmic patterns (a), (b), and (c).

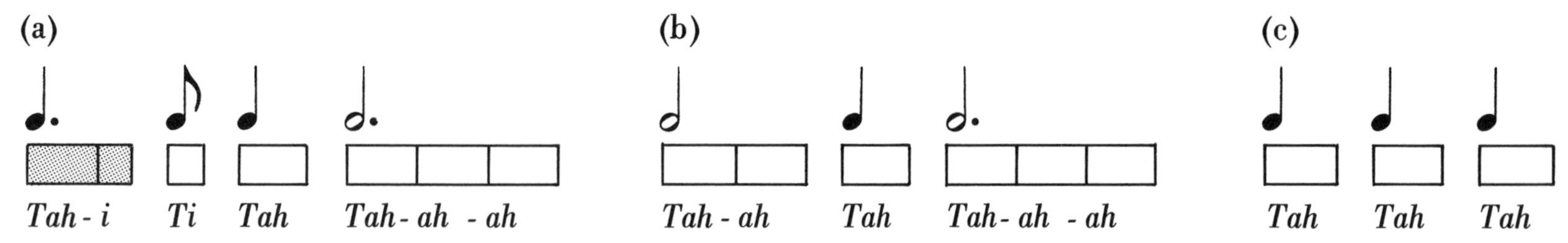

Can you find these rhythmic patterns in "Silent Night"?

2. How many times does each of the following rhythmic patterns appear in "Silent Night"?

3. Copy the first line of "Silent Night" on the staves below. Print the correct letter-name under each note.

Date . . . .

12th LESSON

Silent Night

Franz Gruber
arr. B. B.

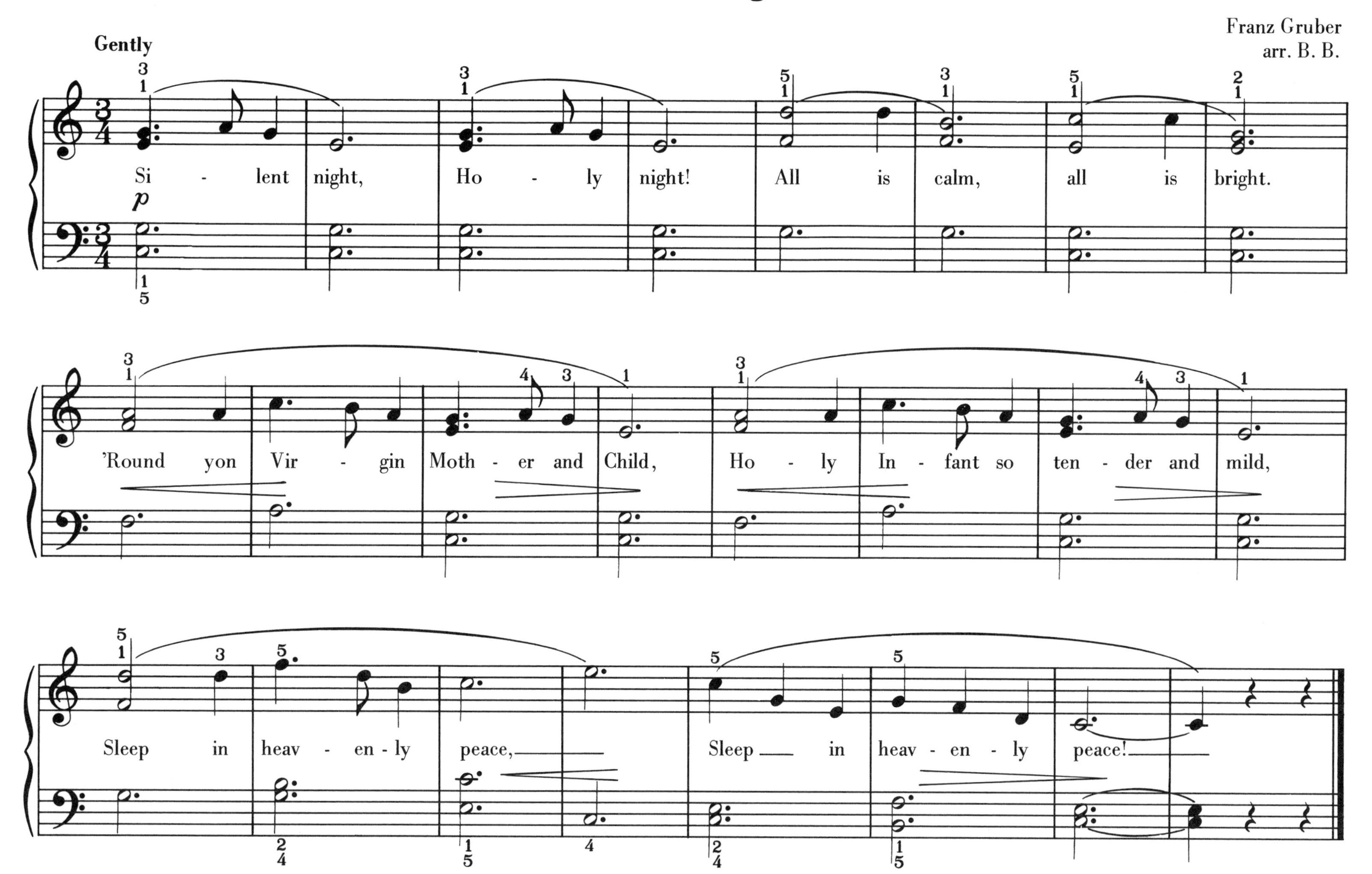

13th LESSON IN WRITING

1. Fill in the blocks for the notes shown below, then copy the notes and clap the rhythmic patterns.

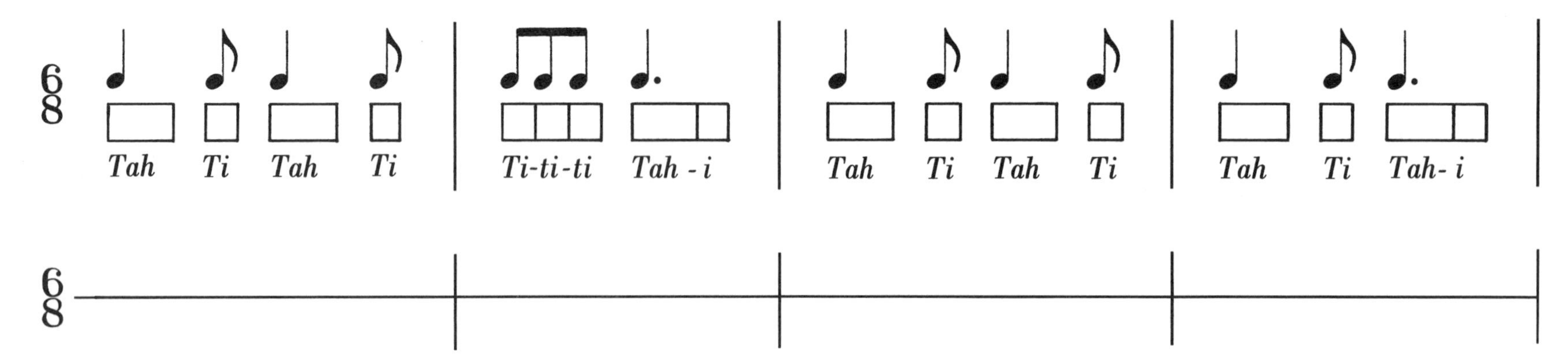

2. Draw bar-lines to divide this tune into measures. Print the correct letter-name under each note, then circle each pair of notes forming a skip (interval).

3. Draw the notes of the scale of C.

Draw the notes of the scale of F.

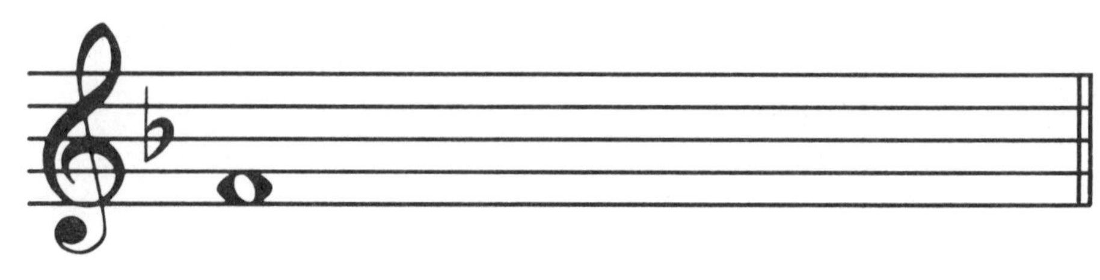

Date . . . .

13th LESSON

En Roulant ma boule

French Folk Song
arr. B. B.

Remember: *8va* - - - - ┐ means to play an octave higher.

14th LESSON IN WRITING

1. Add the time-signature, the missing stems, and the expression marks as found in measures 5 to 8 of "Surprise Symphony". Print the correct letter-name under each note, then write the counts for each measure in the space between the staves. Circle each pair of repeated notes.

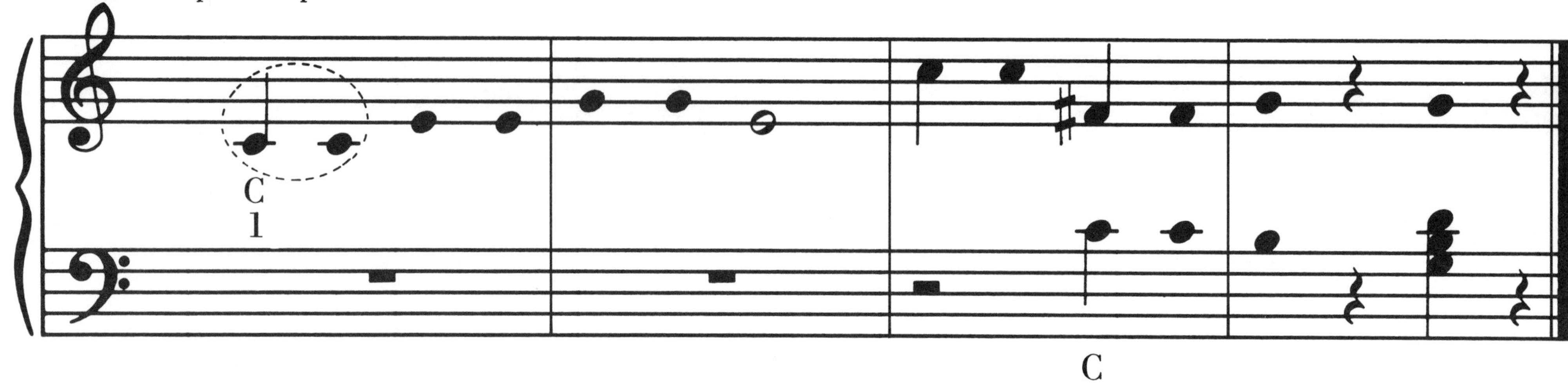

2. Name the skips (intervals) formed by each pair of notes marked by a bracket.

3. Use an X to mark the correct answer. Add an arrow in the direction of each pattern of (a) notes moving UP ; (b) notes moving DOWN ; (c) notes moving UP and DOWN .

Surprise Symphony

Franz Joseph Haydn
arr. B. B.

15th LESSON IN WRITING

1. Copy the opening rhythm of "The Swiss Cuckoo", then clap it while counting the beats aloud. The first eighth note (♪) is an UPBEAT.

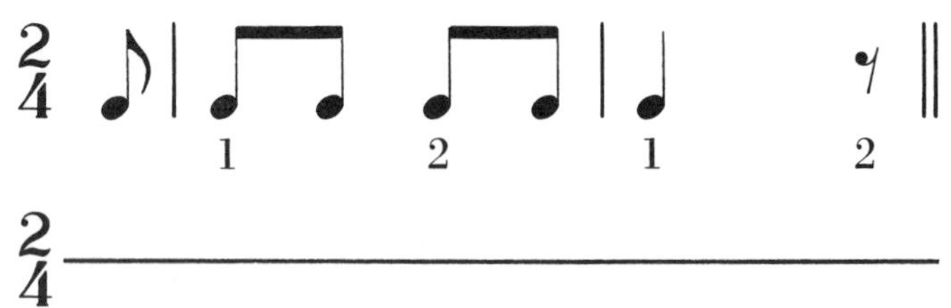

How many times does this rhythmic pattern occur in the right-hand part of "The Swiss Cuckoo"? ________

2. Draw arrows in the direction of (a) notes moving UP ; (b) notes moving DOWN ;
(c) notes moving UP and DOWN ; (d) repeated notes .
Circle and name the 3 skips (intervals) found in these excerpts.

3. Use an X to mark the correct answer.

p	♪	*mf*	crescendo sign	diminuendo sign
loud ☐ soft ☐	eighth note ☐ quarter note ☐	mezzo forte ☐ crescendo ☐	crescendo ☐ diminuendo ☐	mezzo piano ☐ diminuendo ☐

33
Date . . . .
15th LESSON
Eighth rest
The Swiss Cuckoo
Not too slow
B. B.
Note the cuckoo calls in measures 8, 9 and 10.

16th LESSON IN WRITING

1. Draw a note for each letter-name.

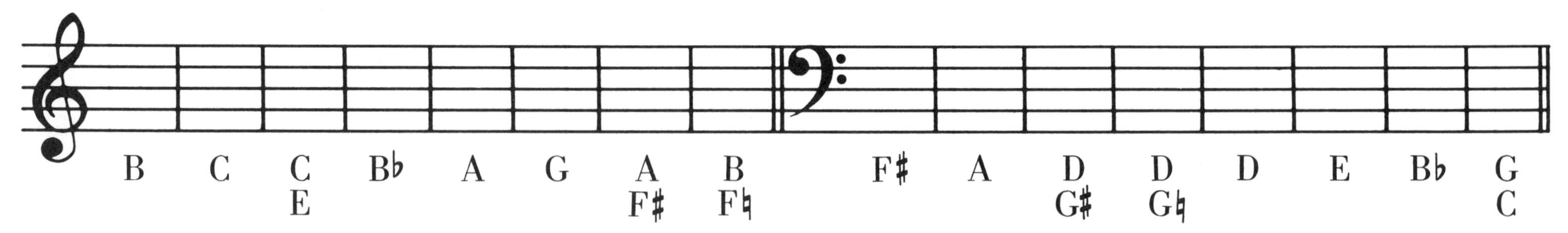

2. Draw notes as directed.

whole note ☐ half note ☐ quarter note ☐ two eighth notes ☐ dotted quarter note ☐ three eighth notes ☐

3. Draw bar-lines to divide this tune into measures.
Write the counts for each measure in the space between the staves, then print the letter-name under each note.
Mark an X above the highest note and an X below the lowest note.
Draw arrows in the direction of note patterns (a), (b), (c), and (d).

4. How many times does the rhythmic pattern ♩|♩ ♩ ♩ ♩|♩ ♩ occur in "On the Merry-Go-Round"? ________

Date ....

16th LESSON

On the Merry-Go-Round

*Play in the usual position, as at the beginning of the piece.
Remember: *8va*-------- means to play an octave higher.

O Canada

The Star-Spangled Banner

The ♩. ♪ rhythm can be played by ear.

ELEMENTARY TECHNIC FOR BEGINNERS

(To build the hand and to develop the player's skill and co-ordination)*

Step 1

FOR FIFTHS

Play this pattern hands separately beginning on every white key, the RIGHT HAND going UP the keyboard, the LEFT HAND going DOWN the keyboard.

Step 2

FOR FIFTHS AND OCTAVE DISPLACEMENTS

Play the pattern shown in *Step 1,* repeating the pattern an octave higher in the RIGHT HAND and an octave lower in the LEFT HAND. Play hands separetely beginning on every white key, going up or down the keyboard.

*These exercises may be given to students in connection with their pieces, at the discretion of the teacher.

Step 3

FOR THIRDS Play each pattern hands separately beginning on every white key, the RIGHT HAND going UP the keyboard, the LEFT HAND going DOWN the keyboard. Use the three fingerings shown.

Step 4

FOR TRIADS Play each triad containing three white keys hands separately. Continue UP the keyboard with the RIGHT HAND and DOWN the keyboard with the LEFT HAND.

This certifies that

____

has completed

PART THREE

of

The A.B.C. of PIANO PLAYING

and is eligible for promotion to

CONSERVATORY GRADE 1 WORK

____
Teacher

____
Date